shaken

shaken

classic cocktails—shaken not stirred

Parragon

Bath · New York · Singapore · Hong Kong · Cologne · Delhi · Melbourne

First published by Parragon in 2007

Parragon
Queen Street House
4 Queen Street
Bath BA1 1HE

Designed by Talking Design
Photography by Mike Cooper
Introduction text and additional recipes by Linda Doeser
Food Styling by Lincoln Jefferson and Carole Handslip

ISBN 978-1-4054-9510-3

Printed in China

WARNING

Recipes containing raw eggs are not suitable for convalescents, the elderly, or pregnant women. Please consume alcohol responsibly.

CONTENTS

introduction

From the classic drinks of the Jazz Age to today's colorful and exotic concoctions, the shaker is the icon of sophistication. Making cocktails isn't difficult and is great fun. Reading the following guidelines should guarantee you have all the skills of a professional bartender at your fingertips.

Bar Essentials

Cocktail shaker The standard type is a 2¼-cup cylindrical container with a double lid incorporating a strainer. The Boston shaker consists of double conical containers without a strainer.

Strainer A bar strainer prevents ice from being poured into the glass. You could use a small nylon strainer.

Jigger This small measuring cup is often double-ended. A standard measure is 1½ oz (3 tbsp). Most jiggers have a 1½-oz cup one end and a ¾-oz cup the other. If you don't have a jigger, use a liqueur, schnapps, or shot glass.

Other basics Lots of ordinary kitchen equipment is useful: corkscrew, measuring cups, citrus juicer, cutting board, kitchen knives, and a citrus zester. You will require an ice bucket and tongs.

Glasses

Balloon wine glass Short-stemmed glass with a large bowl (10 oz)

Cocktail glass Stemmed glass with a cone-shaped bowl (4–5 oz)

Collins glass Tall narrow glass with straight sides (10 oz)

Highball glass Tall straight glass (8 oz)

Margarita glass Stemmed glass with a small bowl topped with a wide saucer shape

Old-fashioned glass Chunky glass (8 oz)

Shot glass Small glass (2 oz)

Bartender's Tips

Shaking cocktails Remove the lid from the shaker, add ice, and pour in the ingredients. Close and shake vigorously for 10–20 seconds, until the outside of the shaker is misty. Remove the small lid and pour the cocktail into the glass. If your shaker doesn't have an integral strainer, use a separate one. It's best not to mix more than 2 servings at a time.

Sugar syrup Professionals use sugar syrup to sweeten cocktails. Put 4 tbsp superfine sugar and 4 tbsp water into a pan. Gradually bring to a boil, stirring. Boil, without stirring, for 1–2 minutes, remove from the heat, and let cool. Store in a sterilized bottle in the refrigerator for up to 2 months.

Chilling glasses Place glasses in the refrigerator for 2 hours before using. Alternatively, fill them with cracked ice, stir well, then tip out the ice before pouring in the cocktail.

Frosting glasses To decorate the rim of a glass, rub it with a little lemon or lime juice and then dip the glass upside down into a shallow saucer of superfine sugar or fine salt.

Ice To crack ice, put cubes in a strong plastic bag and hit with the smooth side of a meat bat or a rolling pin. Alternatively, bang the bag against a wall.

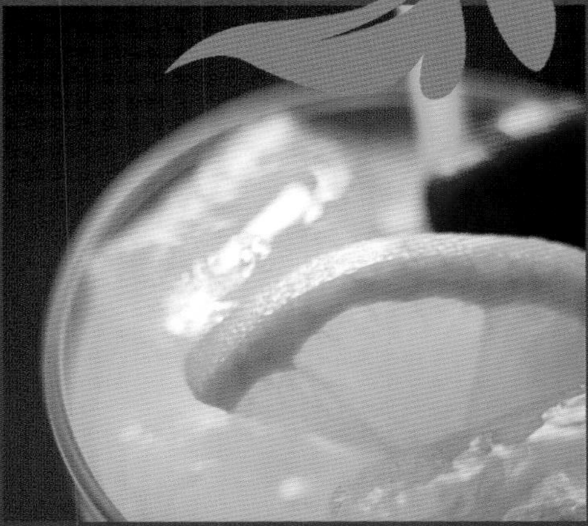

The Classics

Martini

FOR MANY, THIS IS THE ULTIMATE COCKTAIL. IT IS NAMED AFTER ITS INVENTOR, MARTINI DE ANNA DE TOGGIA, NOT THE FAMOUS BRAND OF VERMOUTH! IT CAN VARY HUGELY, FROM THE ORIGINAL (SEE BELOW) TO THE ULTRA DRY, WHEN THE GLASS IS MERELY RINSED OUT WITH VERMOUTH.

SERVES 1
3 measures gin
1 tsp dry vermouth, or to taste
cracked ice cubes
green cocktail olives

1 Pour the gin and vermouth over cracked ice in a mixing glass and stir well to mix.
2 Strain into a chilled glass and dress with a cocktail olive.

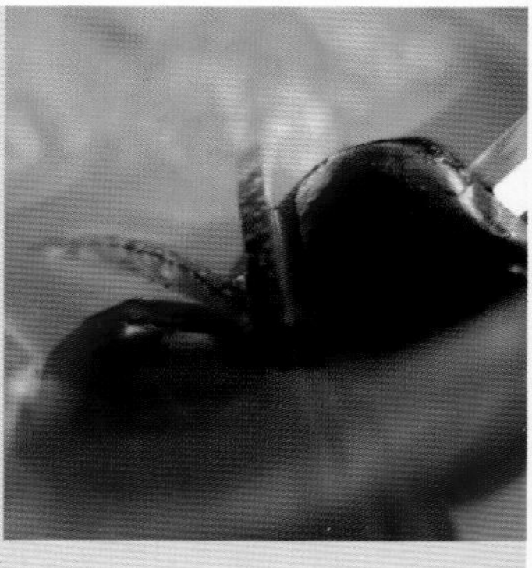

Singapore Sling

IN THE DAYS OF THE BRITISH EMPIRE, THE PRIVILEGED WOULD GATHER AT THEIR EXCLUSIVE CLUBS IN THE RELATIVE COOL OF THE EVENING TO GOSSIP ABOUT THE DAY'S EVENTS. TIMES MAY CHANGE, BUT A SINGAPORE SLING IS STILL THE IDEAL THIRST-QUENCHER ON A HOT SUMMER EVENING.

SERVES 1
2 measures gin
1 measure cherry brandy
1 measure lemon juice
1 tsp grenadine
cracked ice cubes
soda water
lime peel and cocktail cherries

1 Shake the gin, cherry brandy, lemon juice, and grenadine vigorously over ice until well frosted.
2 Half fill a chilled glass with cracked ice cubes and strain in the cocktail.
3 Top up with soda water and dress with lime peel and cocktail cherries.

Manhattan

SAID TO HAVE BEEN INVENTED BY SIR WINSTON CHURCHILL'S AMERICAN MOTHER, JENNIE, THE MANHATTAN IS ONE OF MANY COCKTAILS NAMED AFTER PLACES IN NEW YORK.

SERVES 1
dash of Angostura bitters
3 measures rye whiskey
1 measure sweet vermouth
cracked ice cubes
cocktail cherry, to decorate

1. Shake the liquids over cracked ice in a mixing glass and mix well.
2. Strain into a chilled glass and decorate with the cherry.

Mimosa

SO CALLED BECAUSE IT RESEMBLES THE COLOR OF A MIMOSA'S ATTRACTIVE YELLOW BLOOM.

SERVES 1
flesh of 1 passion fruit
½ measure orange Curaçao
crushed ice
champagne, chilled
slice of star fruit

1. Scoop out the passion fruit flesh into a jug or shaker and shake with the Curaçao and a little crushed ice until frosted.
2. Pour into the base of a champagne flute and top up with champagne.
3. Dress with the slice of star fruit.

Piña Colada

ONE OF THE YOUNGER GENERATION OF CLASSICS, THIS BECAME POPULAR DURING THE COCKTAIL REVIVAL OF THE 1980S AND HAS REMAINED SO EVER SINCE.

SERVES 1

4–6 crushed ice cubes
2 measures white rum
1 measure dark rum
3 measures pineapple juice
2 measures coconut cream
pineapple wedges, to decorate

1. Whizz the crushed ice in a blender with the white rum, dark rum, pineapple juice, and coconut cream until smooth.
2. Pour, without straining, into a tall, chilled glass and dress with pineapple wedges.

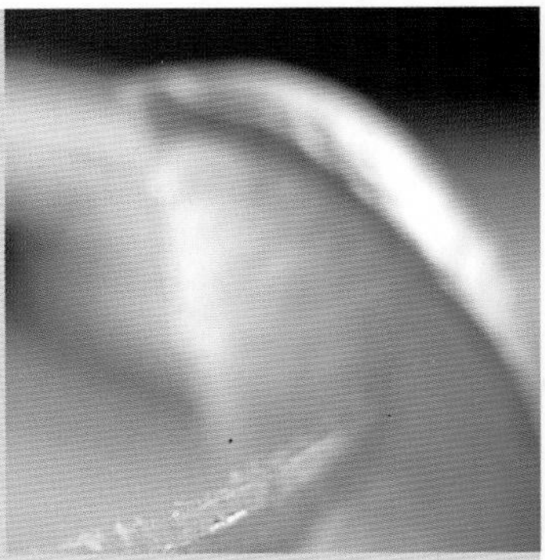

Margarita

THIS COCKTAIL, ATTRIBUTED TO FRANCISCO MORALES AND INVENTED IN 1942 IN MEXICO, IS A MORE CIVILIZED VERSION OF THE ORIGINAL WAY TO DRINK TEQUILA—LICK OF SALT FROM THE BACK OF YOUR HAND, SUCK OF LIME JUICE AND A SHOT OF TEQUILA!

SERVES 1

lime wedge
coarse salt
3 measures white tequila
1 measure Triple Sec or Cointreau
2 measures lime juice
cracked ice cubes
slice of lime, to decorate

1. Rub the rim of a chilled cocktail glass with the lime wedge and then dip in a saucer of coarse salt to frost.
2. Shake the tequila, Triple Sec and lime juice vigorously over cracked ice until well frosted.
3. Strain into the prepared glass and decorate with lime.

Dry Martini

UNLIKE THE MARTINI, THIS DRINK HAS ALMOST NO VERMOUTH IN IT. TRADITIONALISTS WILL TELL YOU SIMPLY TO WAVE THE BOTTLE OVER THE GLASS!

SERVES 1

1 measure London Dry gin
dash of dry vermouth
ice
a single olive on a toothpick

1. Shake the gin and vermouth over a handful of ice until well frosted and combined.
2. Strain into a chilled glass.
3. Decorate simply with a single olive.

Club Mojito

DARK RUM IS RICH IN FLAVOR AND REDOLENT OF SUNSHINE HOLIDAY MEMORIES.

SERVES 1

1 tsp sugar syrup
few mint leaves
juice of ½ lime
ice
2 measures dark rum
soda water
dash of Angostura bitters
mint leaves, to decorate

1. Put the syrup, mint leaves, and lime juice in a glass and crush or muddle the mint leaves.
2. Add ice and rum, then top up with soda water to taste.
3. Finish with a dash of Angostura bitters and a mint leaf.

Sangria

A PERFECT LONG COLD DRINK FOR A CROWD OF FRIENDS AT A SUMMER BARBECUE!

SERVES 6
juice of 1 orange
juice of 1 lemon
2 tbsp powdered sugar
ice cubes
1 orange, thinly sliced
1 lemon, thinly sliced
1 bottle red wine, chilled
lemonade

1. Shake the orange and lemon juice with the sugar and transfer to a large bowl or jug.
2. When the sugar has dissolved, add a few ice cubes, sliced fruit and wine.
3. Marinate for 1 hour if possible, and then add lemonade to taste and more ice.

Tom Collins

THIS COOLING LONG DRINK IS A CELEBRATED COCKTAIL AND WAS THE INSPIRATION OF SEVERAL GENERATIONS OF THE COLLINS DRINKS FAMILY SCATTERED ACROSS THE GLOBE.

SERVES 1

3 measures gin
2 measures lemon juice
½ measure sugar syrup
5–6 cracked ice cubes
soda water
slice of lemon

1 Shake the gin, lemon juice, and sugar syrup vigorously over ice until well frosted.

2 Strain into a tall, chilled tumbler and top up with soda water.

3 Dress with a slice of lemon.

Mai Tai

CREATED IN 1944 BY RESTAURATEUR "TRADER VIC" IT WAS DESCRIBED AS "MAI TAI—ROE AE" MEANING "OUT OF THIS WORLD." IT IS ALWAYS FLAMBOYANTLY DRESSED.

SERVES 1

2 measures white rum
2 measures dark rum
1 measure orange Curaçao
1 measure lime juice
1 tbsp orgeat
1 tbsp grenadine
cracked ice cubes
slices of pineapple, pieces of fruit peel, cocktail cherries and straws, to decorate

1 Shake the white and dark rums, Curaçao, lime juice, orgeat, and grenadine vigorously over ice until well frosted.

2 Strain into a chilled cocktail glass and decorate as you wish.

Hurricane

THIS FLAMBOYANT COCKTAIL IS SYNONYMOUS WITH PAT O'BRIEN'S BAR IN THE NEW ORLEANS FRENCH QUARTER. A POPULAR DRINK WITH THE TOURISTS BECAUSE IF YOU MANAGED TO DRINK IT ALL YOU COULD TAKE YOUR GLASS HOME.

SERVES 1

ice
4 measures dark rum
1 measure lemon juice
2 measures sweet fruit cocktail or juice (passion fruit and orange are the usual)
soda water
slices of orange and cherries

1 Fill a tall cocktail glass or highball glass with ice.

2 Shake the rum and juices until well combined and pour into the chilled glass. Top up with soda water and decorate with the orange slices and cherries.

Daiquiri

DAIQUIRI IS A TOWN IN CUBA, WHERE THIS DRINK WAS SAID TO HAVE BEEN INVENTED IN THE EARLY PART OF THE TWENTIETH CENTURY. A BUSINESSMAN HAD RUN OUT OF IMPORTED GIN AND SO HAD TO MAKE DO WITH THE LOCAL DRINK—RUM—WHICH, AT THAT TIME, WAS OFTEN OF UNRELIABLE QUALITY.

SERVES 1

2 measures white rum
¾ measure lime juice
½ tsp sugar syrup
cracked ice

1. Pour the rum, lime juice, and sugar syrup over ice and shake vigorously until well frosted.
2. Strain into a chilled cocktail glass.

Bellini

THIS DELICIOUS CONCOCTION WAS CREATED BY GIUSEPPE CIPRIANI AT HARRY'S BAR IN VENICE, AROUND 1943.

SERVES 1

1 measure fresh peach juice made from lightly sweetened liquidized peaches
powdered sugar ice
3 measures champagne, chilled

1 Dip the rim of a champagne flute into some peach juice and then into the sugar to create a sugar-frosted effect. Set aside to dry.
2 Shake the peach juice over ice and strain into the champagne flute.
3 Carefully top up with champagne.

The New Wave

Slow Comfortable Screw

ALWAYS USE FRESHLY SQUEEZED ORANGE JUICE TO MAKE THIS REFRESHING COCKTAIL—IT IS JUST NOT THE SAME WITH BOTTLED JUICE. THIS SIMPLE, CLASSIC COCKTAIL HAS GIVEN RISE TO NUMEROUS AND INCREASINGLY ELABORATE VARIATIONS.

SERVES 1
2 measures sloe gin
orange juice
cracked ice cubes
slice of orange

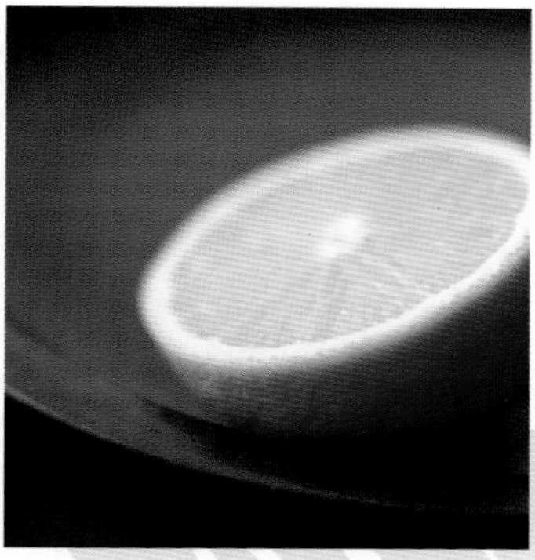

1 Shake the sloe gin and orange juice over ice until well frosted and pour into a chilled glass.
2 Decorate with a slice of orange.

Mint Julep

A JULEP IS SIMPLY A MIXED DRINK SWEETENED WITH SYRUP. THE MINT JULEP WAS PROBABLY FIRST MADE IN THE UNITED STATES, AND IS THE TRADITIONAL DRINK OF THE KENTUCKY DERBY.

SERVES 1
leaves from 1 fresh mint sprig
1 tbsp sugar syrup
crushed ice cubes
3 measures bourbon whiskey
fresh mint sprig, to dress

1 Put the mint leaves and sugar syrup into a small chilled glass and mash with a teaspoon.
2 Add the crushed ice and shake to mix before adding the bourbon.
3 Decorate with the mint sprig.

White Lady

SIMPLE, ELEGANT, SUBTLE, AND MUCH MORE POWERFUL THAN APPEARANCE SUGGESTS, THIS IS THE PERFECT COCKTAIL TO SERVE BEFORE AN AL FRESCO SUMMER DINNER.

SERVES 1

2 measures gin
1 measure Triple Sec
1 measure lemon juice
cracked ice cubes

1. Shake the gin, Triple Sec, and lemon juice vigorously over ice until well frosted.
2. Strain into a chilled cocktail glass.

Kamikaze

NO TURNING BACK ON THIS ONE. IT'S SO DELICIOUS—YOU WON'T BE ABLE TO PUT IT DOWN.

SERVES 1

1 measure vodka
1 measure Triple Sec
½ measure fresh lime juice
½ measure fresh lemon juice
ice
dry white wine, chilled
slices of cucumber

1. Shake the first four ingredients together over ice until well frosted.
2. Strain into a chilled glass and top up with wine.
3. Dress with slices of cucumber.

Nirvana

IT MAY NOT BE POSSIBLE TO OBTAIN A PERFECT STATE OF HARMONY AND BLISS THROUGH A COCKTAIL, BUT THIS HAS TO BE THE NEXT BEST THING.

SERVES 1

2 measures dark rum
½ measure grenadine
½ measure tamarind syrup
1 tsp sugar syrup
ice and cracked ice cubes
grapefruit juice

1. Shake the rum, grenadine, tamarind syrup and sugar syrup, vigorously over ice until well frosted.
2. Half fill a chilled glass with cracked ice cubes and strain the cocktail over them.
3. Top up with grapefruit juice.

Black Widow

NOT AS WICKED AS ITS TITLE SUGGESTS, BUT IF YOU ARE FEELING ADVENTUROUS YOU COULD TAKE IT STRAIGHT, ON THE ROCKS!

SERVES 1

$\frac{2}{3}$ measure dark rum
$\frac{1}{3}$ measure Southern Comfort
juice of 1/2 lime
dash of Curaçao
ice
soda water
lime peel

1 Shake the first four ingredients together well over ice and strain into a chilled tumbler.
2 Top up with soda water to taste and finish with a twist of lime.

Island Blues

THIS TASTE OF THE DEEP BLUE OCEAN COMES FROM THOSE ROMANTIC RUM-PRODUCING ISLANDS.

SERVES 1
lemon juice
powdered sugar
¾ measure peach schnapps
½ measure blue Curaçao
1 small egg white
dash of fresh lemon juice
ice
lemonade

1. Frost the rim of a glass using the lemon juice and sugar. Set aside to dry.
2. Place the next four ingredients into a cocktail shaker half full of ice.
3. Shake well and strain into a glass.
4. Top up with lemonade.

Indian Summer

THE COFFEE LIQUEUR IS THE KEY INGREDIENT IN THIS DELICIOUS LONG MIX—IT WOULD BE GOOD WITH CRÈME DE NOYEAU OR CRÈME DE CACAO TOO.

SERVES 1
1 measure vodka
2 measures Kahlúa
1 measure gin
2 measures pineapple
ice
tonic water

1. Shake the first four ingredients well over ice until frosted.
2. Strain into a medium cocktail glass or wine glass and top up with tonic water to taste.

Ocean Breeze

IT'S A BREEZE TO MAKE AND AS COLORFUL AS THE WHIPPED-UP OCEAN ON AN EARLY MORNING. JUST DON'T DILUTE IT TOO MUCH.

SERVES 1

1 measure white rum
1 measure Amaretto
½ measure blue Curaçao
½ measure pineapple juice
crushed ice
soda water

1 Shake the first four ingredients together over ice.
2 Pour into a tall glass and top up with soda water to taste.

Palm Beach

IF IT'S BEEN A LONG TIME SINCE YOUR LAST HOLIDAY, CONJURE UP THE BLUE SKIES OF FLORIDA AND THE ROLLING SURF WITH THIS SUNNY COCKTAIL.

SERVES 1

1 measure white rum
1 measure gin
1 measure pineapple juice
cracked ice cubes

1. Shake the rum, gin, and pineapple juice vigorously over ice until well frosted.
2. Strain into a chilled glass.

Whiskey Sour

ORIGINATING IN THE AMERICAN SOUTH AND USING SOME OF THE BEST AMERICAN WHISKEY, THIS CLASSIC CAN ALSO BE MADE WITH VODKA, GIN OR OTHER SPIRITS.

SERVES 1

1 measure lemon or lime juice
2 measures blended whiskey
1 tsp sugar syrup
slice of lemon or lime
maraschino cherry

1. Shake the first three ingredients well over ice and strain into a cocktail glass.
2. Finish with a slice of lemon or lime and a cherry.

Blood and Sand

CHERRY BRANDY IS QUITE A FULL-FLAVORED LIQUEUR. YOU COULD USE BRANDY INSTEAD, BUT DO NOT EXPECT AS PUNCHY A COCKTAIL.

SERVES 1

1 measure Scotch
1 measure cherry brandy
1 measure red vermouth
ice
orange juice

1 Shake the first three ingredients over ice until frosted.
2 Strain into a medium-size glass and top up with orange juice.

Fat Man Running

BLUE CURAÇAO CAN MAKE BEAUTIFUL COCKTAILS OF STRANGE COLORS—YOU MAY FIND YOU PREFER TO USE A CLEAR CURAÇAO IN THIS COCKTAIL!

SERVES 1
2 measures dark rum
½ measure blue Curaçao
½ measure lime juice
ice cubes
ginger ale

1 Whizz all the ingredients except the ginger ale in a blender on fast speed for about 10 seconds.
2 Pour into a tall glass and shake before topping up with ginger ale.

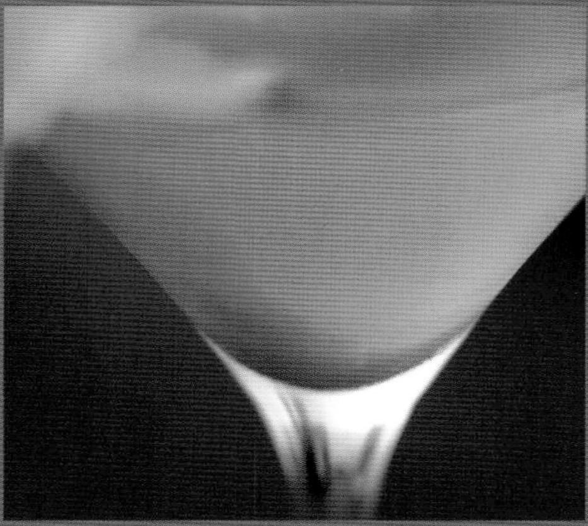

The Perfect Pick-Me-Up

The Blues

THIS BRIGHT COCKTAIL WOULD BE QUITE SWEET IF IT WEREN'T FOR THE LEMON JUICE, SO BE CAREFUL WITH THE BALANCE OF THE INGREDIENTS THE FIRST TIME YOU MAKE IT.

SERVES 1

1½ measures tequila
½ measure maraschino
½ measure blue Curaçao
½ measure lemon juice
ice cubes
bitter lemon

1 Shake the first four ingredients well over ice until frosted.
2 Strain into a tumbler and top up with bitter lemon.

Huatusco Whammer

TO BE AUTHENTIC, THIS COCKTAIL SHOULD BE TOPPED UP WITH COCA-COLA, BUT YOU CAN USE OTHER BRANDS OF COLA IF YOU PREFER. MAKE SURE THAT THE COLA IS WELL CHILLED BEFORE ADDING IT.

SERVES 1

1 measure white tequila
½ measure white rum
½ measure vodka
½ measure gin
½ measure Triple Sec
1 measure lemon juice
½ tsp sugar syrup
cracked ice cubes
cola

1. Shake the tequila, rum, vodka, gin, Triple Sec, lemon juice, and sugar syrup vigorously over ice until well frosted.
2. Fill a chilled glass with cracked ice cubes and strain the cocktail over them.
3. Top up with cola, stir gently and serve with straws if liked.

Zander

A LIQUORICE-FLAVORED LIQUEUR, SAMBUCA IS TRADITIONALLY DRUNK STRAIGHT, BUT ITS INTENSE FLAVOR IS GREAT WITH FRUIT DRINKS, AND MAKES A CHANGE FOR A LONG DRINK.

SERVES 1

1 measure Sambuca
1 measure orange juice
dash of lemon juice
ice
bitter lemon

1 Shake the first three ingredients over ice and strain into a glass filled with ice.
2 Top up with bitter lemon.

White Cosmopolitan

NOTHING LIKE ITS PINK COUSIN THE COSMOPOLITAN, FOR THIS IS FAR MORE FRUITY AND INSTEAD OF VODKA, IT IS BASED ON A PUNCHY LEMON-FLAVORED LIQUEUR.

SERVES 1
1½ measures Limoncello
½ measure Cointreau
1 measure white cranberry and grape juice
ice
dash of orange bitters
few red cranberries

1. Shake the first three ingredients over ice until well frosted.
2. Strain into a chilled glass.
3. Add a dash of bitters and dress with cranberries.

Charleston

THIS LITTLE NUMBER COMBINES SEVERAL TASTES AND FLAVORS TO PRODUCE A VERY LIVELY DRINK. DON'T DRINK IT WHEN YOU ARE THIRSTY—YOU MIGHT WANT TOO MANY!

SERVES 1

¼ measure gin
¼ measure dry vermouth
¼ measure sweet vermouth
¼ measure Cointreau
¼ measure kirsch
¼ measure maraschino
ice
twist of lemon, to decorate

1 Shake all the liquids together well over ice and strain into a chilled glass.
2 Dress with a twist of lemon.

Pink Squirrel

CRÈME DE NOYEAU HAS A WONDERFUL, SLIGHTLY BITTER, NUTTY FLAVOR, BUT IS, IN FACT, MADE FROM PEACH AND APRICOT KERNELS. IT IS USUALLY SERVED AS A LIQUEUR, BUT DOES COMBINE WELL WITH SOME OTHER INGREDIENTS IN COCKTAILS.

SERVES 1

2 measures dark crème de cacao
1 measure crème de noyeau
1 measure light cream
cracked ice cubes

1. Shake the crème de cacao, crème de noyeau, and light cream vigorously over ice until well frosted.
2. Strain into a chilled glass.

Deauville Passion

DEAUVILLE WAS ELEGANT, EXTRAVAGANT, AND VERY FASHIONABLE DURING THE COCKTAIL ERA EARLY LAST CENTURY AND NO DOUBT MANY GREAT COCKTAILS WERE CREATED THERE.

SERVES 1

1¾ measures cognac
1¼ measures apricot Curaçao
1¼ measures passion fruit juice
ice
bitter lemon to taste
mint leaves

1 Shake the first three ingredients over ice until well frosted.
2 Strain into a chilled glass, top up with bitter lemon to taste and dress with mint leaves.

Zombie

THE INDIVIDUAL INGREDIENTS OF THIS COCKTAIL, INCLUDING LIQUEURS AND FRUIT JUICES, VARY CONSIDERABLY FROM ONE RECIPE TO ANOTHER, BUT ALL ZOMBIES CONTAIN A MIXTURE OF WHITE, GOLDEN, AND DARK RUM IN A RANGE OF PROPORTIONS.

SERVES 4

2 measures dark rum
2 measures white rum
1 measure golden rum
1 measure Triple Sec
1 measure lime juice
1 measure orange juice
1 measure pineapple juice
1 measure guava juice
1 tbsp grenadine
1 tbsp orgeat
1 tsp Pernod
crushed ice cubes
sprigs of fresh mint and pineapple wedges

1 Shake all the liquids together over crushed ice until well combined and frosted.

2 Pour without straining into a chilled cocktail glass.

3 Dress with mint and a wedge of pineapple.

Adam 'n' Eve

DON'T EXPECT THIS COCKTAIL TO BE FULL OF APPLES! THE BASE IS SHARP AND ASTRINGENT, WHILE THE TOP IS SWEET AND FROTHY–NO DISCRIMINATION HERE, OF COURSE!

SERVES 1

2 measures Triple Sec
1 measure vodka
1 measure grapefruit juice
1 measure cranberry juice
ice
5–6 cubes pineapple
2 tsp powdered sugar
crushed ice
strawberry

1. Shake the first four ingredients over ice until well frosted.
2. Strain into a chilled glass.
3. In a blender whizz the pineapple with the sugar and 1–2 tbsp of crushed ice to a frothy slush.
4. Float gently on the top of the cocktail.
5. Dress with a slice of strawberry.

Martinez

THE ORIGINAL RECIPE MAY GO BACK TO 1849 AND WAS MADE WITH AN AMERICAN GIN CALLED OLD TOM WHICH WAS SLIGHTLY SWEETENED.

SERVES 1
2 measures iced gin
1 measure Italian vermouth
dash of Angostura bitters
dash of maraschino
ice cubes
twist or slice of lemon

1. Shake the first four ingredients over ice until frosted.
2. Strain into a chilled cocktail glass and dress with a twist of lemon.

Orange Blossom

DURING THE PROHIBITION YEARS IN THE USA GIN WAS OFTEN QUITE LITERALLY MADE IN THE BATHTUB AND FLAVORED WITH FRESH ORANGE JUICE TO CONCEAL ITS FILTHY FLAVOR. MADE WITH GOOD-QUALITY GIN, WHICH NEEDS NO SUCH CONCEALMENT, THIS DRINK IS DELIGHTFULLY REFRESHING.

SERVES 1

2 measures gin
2 measures orange juice
cracked ice cubes
slice of orange, to decorate

1 Shake the gin and orange juice vigorously over ice until well frosted.
2 Strain into a chilled cocktail glass and decorate with the orange slice.

Moonlight

THIS LIGHT WINE-BASED COCKTAIL IS IDEAL TO MAKE FOR SEVERAL PEOPLE.

SERVES 4
3 measures grapefruit juice
4 measures gin
1 measure kirsch
4 measures white wine
½ tsp lemon zest
ice

1 Shake the first five ingredients well over ice and strain into chilled glasses.

Apple Classic

APPLE LOVERS AND CIDER MAKERS WILL PUT THIS TOP OF THEIR LIST, BUT IT IS DEFINITELY BETTER MADE WITH SWEET RATHER THAN DRY CIDER.

SERVES 1

½ measure gin
½ measure brandy
½ measure Calvados
ice
sweet cider
slice of apple

1 Shake the first three ingredients over ice until frosted.
2 Strain into a medium or tall glass and top up with cider to taste.
3 Dress with a slice of apple.

Cherry Kitch

THIS IS A VELVETY SMOOTH COCKTAIL, FRUITY BUT WITH A RICH BRANDY UNDERTONE. A TOUCH OF MARASCHINO LIQUEUR ADDED AT THE END WOULD BE GOOD, TOO.

SERVES 1

1 measure cherry brandy
2 measures pineapple juice
½ measure kirsch
1 egg white
1 scoop crushed ice
frozen maraschino cherry

1 Shake the first four ingredients well over ice until frosted.

2 Pour into a chilled tall thin glass and top with a frozen maraschino cherry.

index